SECURE YOUR SUCCESS!: A GUIDE TO PLANNING EVENTS LIKE A BOSS!

TWANITA DOZIER

~

This book is dedicated to:

Maury Dozier

Zavier Brooks Dozier

Alijah Brownlee

~

~

PRELUDE

~

"In July of 2018, I hosted my first social networking event in Chicago,

IL. My event catered to small businesses, that were looking for an

opportunity to network & showcase their products and services.

Without any guidance or prior experience with planning an event, my

event was successful and provided a great experience for my guests.

Upon reflection of my experience, I wanted to write a book composed of

knowledge and tips that I learned and believe can help make any event

successful. This book was written and based on my overall planning

experience, which I am sure will provide the guidance that I didn't have.

I hope that you enjoy this book and I wish your next event nothing but

success!"

~ Twanita Dozier ~

Table Of Contents

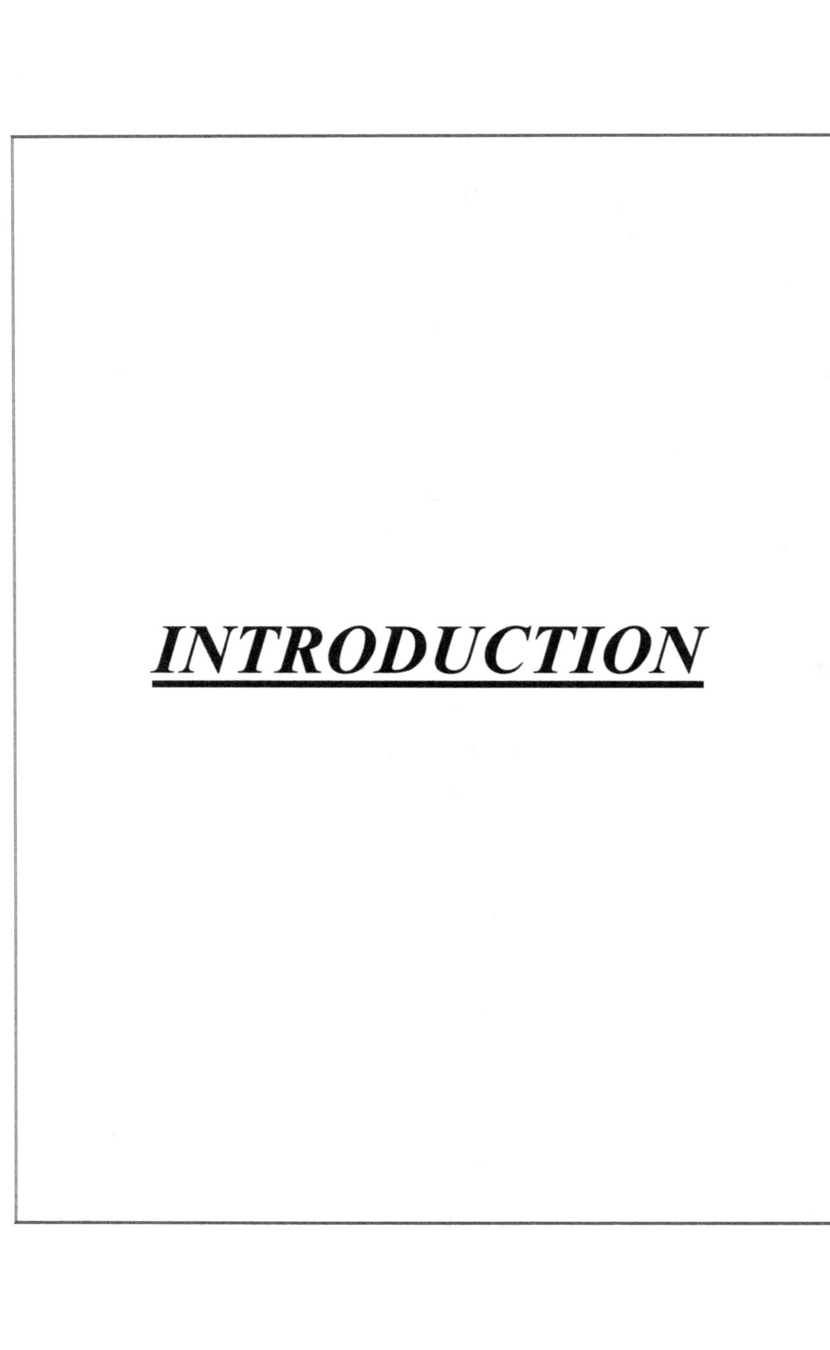

INTRODUCTION

Events are all about having fun and creating memories. Whether your event is a private or public one, it will be an occasion that will be discussed for years to come – so you want to make sure that it is a joyous and unforgettable one. Have you recently considered putting an event together but just aren't sure where to start? Are you already planning an event but feel overwhelmed? Planning an event takes a lot of work and pre-planning, but don't fret as this guide will assist you in the process.

Tip: Purchase a planner for organized planning.

There are eight main keys to planning an event:

Date Selection

Venue Selection

Time Management

Event Advertising

Ticket Pricing

Event Vendors

Event Sponsors

Media Coverage

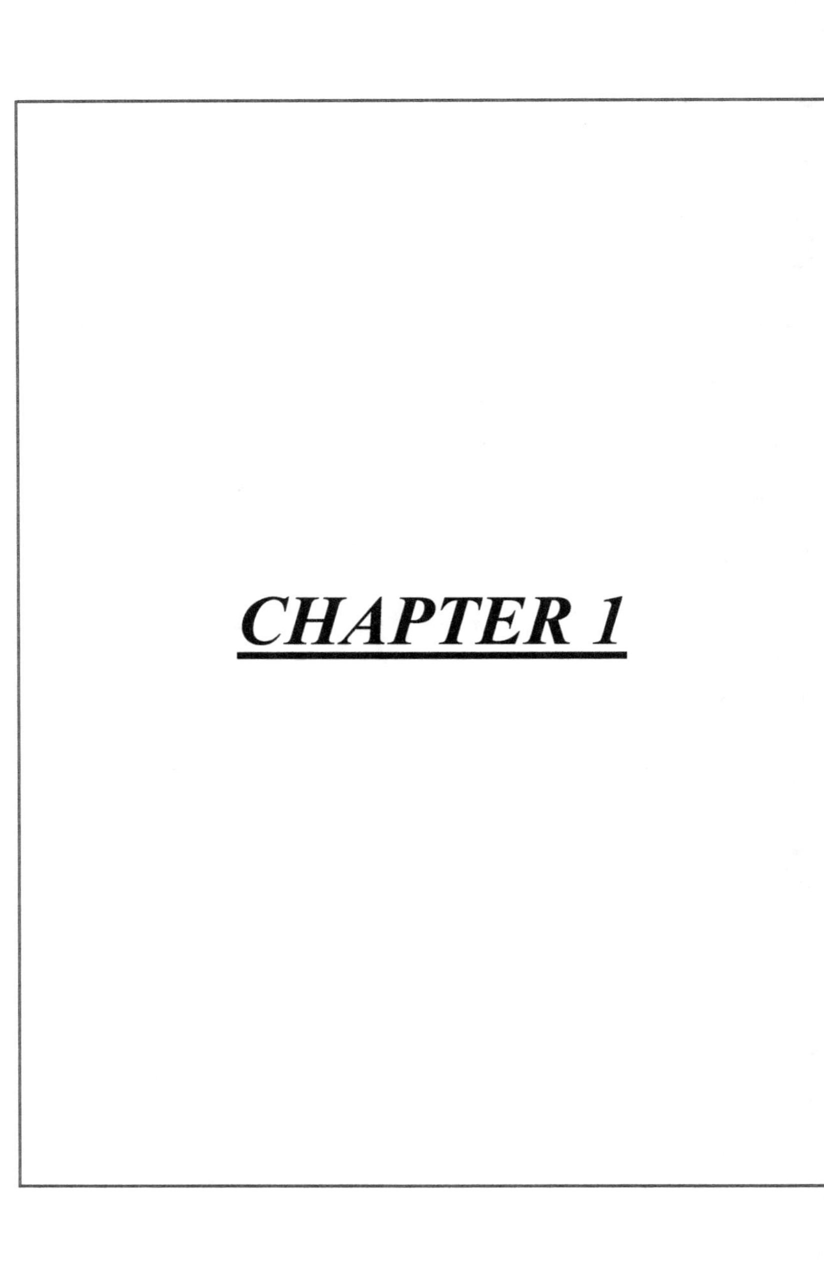

CHAPTER 1

<u>*Date Selection*</u>

When planning your event, you want to make sure that you pick the perfect date! The date that you select plays a huge part in your event and can have a domino effect in the planning process. Here are some things to consider:

Season & Weather
Venue Pricing
Holidays
Major Events & Festivals

Season & Weather: Depending on your event and the season, you want to ensure that they complement each other. You wouldn't want to have a rooftop party in September, as it may be too cold! If your event is geared to accommodate the general public, you want to also take into account the weather for that day.

For example: If you're planning an "outdoor" party during the month of June, you may want to make sure you take into consideration the possibility of any inclement weather. If it decides to rain on the day of

Another thing to keep in mind are the various venue seasons such as: peak, off-peak, prom, wedding, and graduation. This will affect the date of your event, as it will be based on your venue availability and pricing.

Venue Pricing: Depending on the month and day of the week, venue prices will vary. It may be financially beneficial for you to avoid having your event on Friday or Saturday. Usually, venues will charge more money for an event to take place on the weekend (mainly Friday & Saturday) versus during the week. Most venues (not all) will have cheaper pricing for events held Sunday - Thursday. Make sure you have compared pricing to other venues, as it will help you decide what's within your budget, which is based on what you're looking for and the offered price.

Tip: Look at venues that offer specials – as the pricing tends to be heavily discounted.

Holidays: Unless your event has a holiday based theme. (i.e. Children's Christmas Party, Mother's Day Brunch, etc), STAY AWAY FROM HOLIDAYS! Planning events around holidays can either help or hurt your event. Most people will already have plans for the holiday, which in turn can affect your ticket sales and event attendance rate. If your event does not have a holiday based theme, DO NOT PLAN EVENTS AROUND HOLIDAYS! If you're brave enough to plan an event during this time anyway – GO FOR IT!

Major Events & Festivals: When planning your event, you want to make sure you're familiar with the city your event will be held in, as well as the events that may take place during the time of your event. Planning an event when a popular or major event is taking place can ultimately affect your event.

For example: New Orleans usually has a HUGE event called the Essence Festival, which usually takes place in the month of July This is a huge and popular event that attracts thousands of people to New Orleans. Most people going to New Orleans for the Essence Festival have already pre-planned their weekend, to mainly attend Essence

Festival driven events and activities.

I say that to say that planning an event around a major event or festival is NOT a good idea and can hurt your event attendance and ticket sales. However, if you're brave enough to plan an event during this time anyway – GO FOR IT!

Venue Selection

Selecting a venue can be time consuming and difficult, if you allow it! Make sure you do your research well in advance, as it will help you avoid last minute decisions – that can ultimately turn out to be the wrong decision.

Tip: You can browse and rent unique venue spaces via

www.peerspace.com

Your venue selection plays a role in your guest attendance, venue pricing, ticket sales, and overall event success. When selecting your venue, make sure you are selecting a venue that:

Is within your budget

Is available on your desired date

Has a good location

Can accommodate all expected guests (plus some)

Has a good reputation

Has good customer service

Doesn't have hidden fees

Gives you time to change your mind

Is well kept

Offers extras

Is within your budget: A budget is a great way to stay organized and disciplined in planning your event. By giving yourself a budget, you're making sure that you aren't taking on more than you can handle financially. To avoid choosing the wrong venue, you'll want to research and compare venue prices before committing to just one. You wouldn't want to book a venue that you ultimately can't afford, so do your research!

Is available on your desired date: If you have a date in mind, make sure that your desired venue is available on that date. It's always a good idea to ask if the date is available before going to see the venue, to prevent you and the venue from wasting each other's time. If your desired date isn't available, and your event date is flexible, you may want to ask if there is an alternative date available instead.

Has a good location: Having your event in a good location is KEY! If guests think that attending your event will cause them a hassle in any form, they are more likely not to attend. Parking and accessibility are the top reasons why a guest would decide not to attend your event, so make sure your venue has feasible and available parking, as well as being accessible via public transportation.

Offers extras (i.e furniture, free parking, etc): When setting a budget and booking a venue, it's important to consider additional expenses. It's always a great idea to inquire on what all the venue offers, so that you can design your budget accordingly. Some venues offer the space itself as well as chairs and tables, which is perfect because it eliminates an extra expense for you. So if you like a venue and it offers extras at no extra charge, TAKE IT!

Can accommodate all expected guests (plus some): If you have a certain number of guests you would like for the event to accommodate, it's always a great idea to incorporate extra numbers into your count. This will help with last minute ticket sales, so having a venue that is spacious is always great!

Has a good reputation: A bad reputation can hinder any positive or successful thing a venue has done in the past. If your desired venue is known to have a bad reputation, your ticket sales can take a huge hit. Make sure you do your research and read reviews BEFORE booking your venue. This will help you in the long run and prevent any unwanted surprises.

Has good customer service: Good customer service is the key to a successful business overall. If you find that the customer service initially provided to you is not good, chances are that the customer service for your guests will be the same or worse. Make sure you are being proactive and not reactive, as you never want your guests to leave your event unhappy. If guests leave unhappy, they are more likely not to attend any of your future events, as well as tell their loved ones not to attend them either.

Doesn't have hidden fees: Make sure you inquire about ALL fees associated with booking your venue, as you don't want to get your contract and find a fee that wasn't discussed. Hidden fees can be a setback, push you out of your budget, and possibly cause you to look elsewhere. And if you don't have a back-up plan, you'll be back at square one of finding a venue.

Gives you time to change your mind: You always want to set yourself up for success, so it's always a great idea to have three choices of desired venues; this will allow you to have a backup in case one is not available. Be sure you've looked into the amount of time the venue gives you to cancel your booking BEFORE losing your deposit. It's ideal to keep your original venue to avoid losing your deposit – as most are non-refundable. Things happen however - so make sure you're prepared!

Is well kept: It is very important that you do a walk-through of your desired venue, to ensure the venue is worth the cost. Make sure the venue is clean, spacious, and visually appealing, because your venue will set the tone of your event. You want your guests to be comfortable, not turned off – as this can lead to bad press and guests not attending future events.

Time Management

As you're planning your event, you want to spend your time wisely to avoid feeling overwhelmed. To help keep you focused and organized, I recommend having the following:

Event checklist
Planner
Goal list

Event checklist: An event check list will help you stay organized throughout your planning process and eliminate last minute rushing. When creating your event checklist, make sure you are considering everything necessary for your event - big or small.

Checklist examples: Finding a decorator, booking a DJ, ordering chairs.

Planner: A planner will give you a place to view and schedule your event tasks, which can decrease the chances of things being forgotten or overlooked. It is a great idea to plan out your days leading up to your event, as it will help eliminate the chances of you becoming overwhelmed. If there are things you can do in between tasks, DO THEM! It's better to be ahead of things, than behind.

For example: Oct. 1ˢᵗ: Complete venue walk-through.

Oct. 15ᵗʰ: Pay venue deposit.

Oct. 20ᵗʰ: Meet with DJ.

Goal list: A goal list is a great way to manage your event goals, hold yourself accountable, and keep track of things that have already been accomplished. Don't forget to assign goal deadlines, as they will help keep you focused and disciplined.

Goal examples: Staying under a $2000 venue budget, selling 25 pre-sale tickets, getting three event sponsors.

If you feel that you can't do it all alone, it's okay to ask for help! This will actually help you with your time management and eliminate stress.

Tip: Did you know that you can hire a virtual assistant via **www.fiverr.com** *?*

CHAPTER 2

<u>*Event Advertising*</u>

So now that you've selected an event date and booked a venue – YOU NEED TO ADVERTISE YOUR EVENT AND SELL TICKETS! When advertising your event, you want to consider the following things:

Social Media
Pre-Sale Tickets
Sales & Discounts
Influencers
Word of Mouth

Tip: You can advertise your event and sale tickets on

<u>*www.eventbrite.com*</u>

Social Media: Social media is a GREAT tool for advertising, if used correctly. When using social media to advertise your event, make sure you are posting during the most interactive times of the day. This will increase visibility of your event, which can lead to more ticket sales. Sites like Twitter, Facebook, and Instagram provide the option of utilizing paid promotions, which can be customized to your liking and budget.

If you're an avid social media user, it may be safe to say that most of your followers and friends are those you know personally. With you knowing them personally, they may be more opt to supporting your event by attending and/or helping you spread the word to their following. This can consist of sending messages, tagging their friends, and reposting your event details on their profiles.

Tip: Join a few Instagram and Facebook engagement pods. These can help with generating views and leads for your event and your business overall.

Don't forget about #HASHTAGS!! Hashtags are a sure fire way to get your posts seen, especially on sites like Instagram. And if used correctly, hashtags can really help you with advertising your event. If you follow profiles with large followings, take a look at the hashtags they're using and use the ones that would be relevant to your event.

For example: #HoustonEvents, #PopUpShop, #SmallBusiness.

Don't forget about blogs and digital magazines! With technology being so advanced and essential, blogs and magazines can help play a role in advertising your event. There are some people who pay for magazine subscriptions and follow blogs faithfully, so make sure you don't count these resources out. It may actually be a good idea to reach out to the magazine or blogger yourself, to inquire about advertising options for your event.

Tip: Promoting with Boss Up Magazine is a great way to advertise your event and gain exposure. You can check them out via **www.bossupmag.org**.

Pre-Sale Tickets: This is a great way to gain insight on the interest level of your event, as well as sell tickets overall. Pre-Sale tickets are good to hold 1-3 weeks prior to your event, with only having a limited amount available. People who enjoy a good deal and like to plan ahead will usually participate in the option of pre-sale tickets. Pre-Sale tickets are usually cheaper than the original ticket price, may have a promo code, and have an incentive to it.

For example: Use promo code "EARLY" to get a $15 ticket with a free t-shirt. ($35 value)

Want to really spark a sense of urgency with your pre-sale tickets? Use these following words to help:

Limited Time Only!
Act Now!
Special Offer!

Sales & Discounts: Who doesn't like a good sale or discount? Depending on the amount of people your event caters to and your proposed profit goal, it may be a great idea to hold a few ticket sales and discounts. This will help jog sales and build the presence of your event overall. If you're using sources outside of social media, be sure to include a discount code from the source, for tracking and to encourage ticket sales. (applicable). Remember, people love a good deal and discount!

Influencers: Influencers are a big deal and can definitely help anyone who has a business or event. Influencers are people on social media who have a very large following and are considered influential to their audience. When seeking out an influencer to help promote your event,

make sure you are selecting someone who will be beneficial to you.
Take into account their location, their audience, and their content – as
this will help you decide if they are the right influencer for you!

Word Of Mouth: Even though social media is now the new norm, some people aren't too interested or savvy in social media. This in turn causes them to rely more so on sources outside of social media, which can actually be very beneficial for your event. The use of word of mouth is very powerful and can assist in making a successful event. If you know people do not use social media, but are well connected in other ways, ask them to help you spread the word about your event. This can be in a form of text messaging, emails, phone calls, verbally, and giving them your business cards and event flyers.

Other sources of word of mouth are newspapers, radio, and bulletin boards. You may want to consider utilizing these sources, especially various community boards in restaurants, libraries, and other places of business. Usually, when people see flyers or business cards that spark their interest, they are more likely to share it with their loved ones and possibly make an inquiry for more information.

*Tip: Did you know you can create advertising material on **www.staples.com** and pick them up the same day? Just make sure you place your order by 2:00pm.*

Media Coverage

If you plan to have future events, you want to make sure you have media coverage at your event! Media coverage is vital for your event as it adds a professional touch, provides you with footage that can assist in promoting future events, and can help ticket sales overall. Depending on the media coverage company you select, they may incorporate advertising in your fee. Having your media coverage company advertise your event can help build awareness of your event and drive ticket sales, so be sure to inquire about this when selecting your media coverage company.

Tip: Consider utilizing a blogger that offers event coverage. They tend to have a good social media following, may be very well connected, and can provide you with more event exposure. Depending on their following size and audience, this can be a huge help with advertising and ticket sales of your event.

CHAPTER 3

<u>*Ticket Pricing*</u>

If you plan to sell tickets to your event, you want to make sure they are affordable and profitable. Depending on what your event will offer to its guests, there are a few things to keep in mind when deciding on ticket pricing. Here are a list of things to consider:

Venue Fee & Capacity
Food & Drinks
Entertainment
Event Purpose

Venue Fee & Capacity: Depending on how much you paid for your venue, you will need to consider making some kind of profit. Make sure you keep in mind the max capacity of your venue, as that will determine how many tickets you can sell and the necessary pricing.

Food & Drinks: If you're going to offer your guests food and drinks, you want to make sure that you include that expense in your ticket pricing. This usually works well if your guests feel they are getting a good deal for their money.

For example: $35 for endless mimosas and full brunch menu.

Depending on the type of event you're planning, having food and drinks available will help with ticket sales and attendance. What's better than attending an event with food and drinks at your fingertips?!

Entertainment: Having entertainment at your event can increase your ticket sales, as it gives guests an incentive to attend. If guests are really interested in seeing the entertainment offered, they are more likely to purchase tickets and tell their loved ones to do the same. Also, if you're having upscale entertainment, it is important that you also include that into your ticket pricing as well. This will help you make some form of profit of what you've invested into your event.

For example: Celebrity guests, performers, comedians, etc.

Event Purpose: This is really important to keep in mind, as it will actually determine the success of your event ticket sales. Depending on the kind of event you're having, you want to make sure that the ticket prices are appropriate. If ticket prices are too high for the kind of event you're having, people will question if your event is worth attending.

Remember, people want to make sure that they are getting a good deal for their money. However, if you're offering extras with your event, that may play a role in ticket pricing.

For example: $50 for a celebrity meet and greet & autographed photo.

For example: $40 for a business workshop that includes lunch and

goodie bags.

<u>*Event Vendors*</u>

Depending on the type of event you're having, it may be a great idea to incorporate vendors. Having event vendors can add interest to your event, as well as help eliminate YOUR expenses for the event overall. If you're considering having vendors at your event, make sure that you are charging a vendor fee that is fair and affordable. Vendors are less likely to pay to participate in an event that is too expensive. so make sure that the price is right!

Event Sponsors are great to consider, as they too help eliminate YOUR expenses. Again, depending on the type of event you're having, event sponsors can be very beneficial for your event overall. When a business agrees to be an event sponsor, they believe the event is worth investing in and beneficial for their business. Usually, an event sponsor is looking for more business exposure and possibly a tax write off. So the next time you are planning an event, you may want to consider accepting a sponsor!

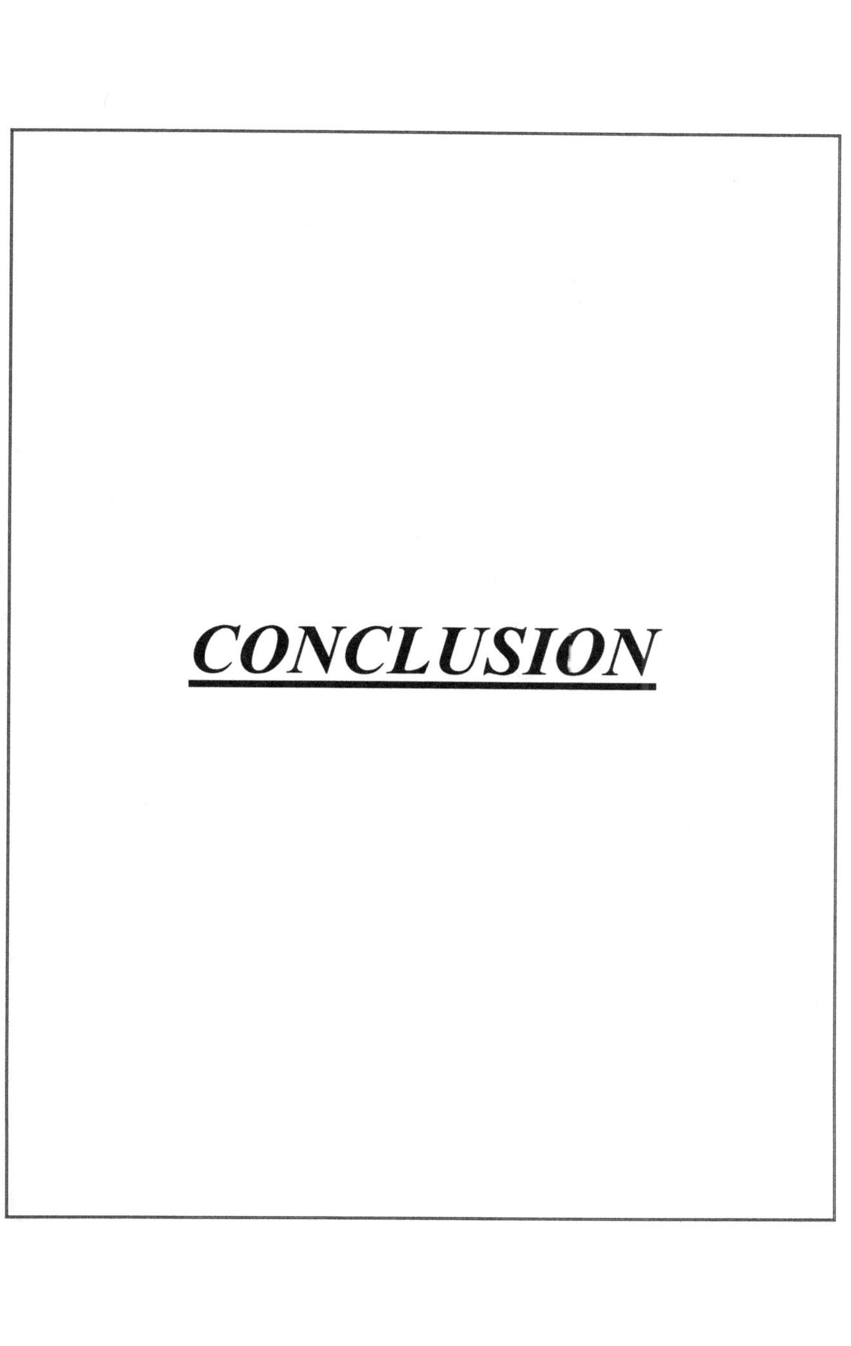

CONCLUSION

There are a lot of steps with event planning, as well as things to consider

throughout the process. If you allow it, event planning can become

overwhelming and frustrating. To help alleviate your frustration, I

suggest planning your event strategically and well in advance.

Remember, you want to give your self room for error and change! If

you're thinking about planning an event or have already started the

planning process, be sure to utilize this guide to help secure your

success!

HAPPY PLANNING!

RESOURCES

Below is a list of places where you can promote your event online.

Please be advised that some of the sites listed carry a fee.

Attend: **http://www.attend.com/**

Craigslist: **https://www.craigslist.org/about/sites**

Cvent: **https://www.cvent.com/**

Event Crazy: **https://www.eventcrazy.com/**

Eventbee: **http://www.eventbee.com/**

Eventbrite: **https://www.eventbrite.com/**

Eventful: **https://www.eventful.com**

Events Get: **https://eventsget.com/**

Events Near Here: **https://www.eventsnearhere.com/post-an-event-free**

Events.org: **https://events.org/**

Eventsetter: **http://www.eventsetter.com/**

Evvnt: **https://evvnt.com/**

Facebook: **https://www.facebook.com/** - **Must be done via your profile or business page.**

In The Calendar: **http://www.inthecalendar.com/**

Instagram: **https://www.instagram.com** – Must be done via your profile.

LinkedIn: **https://www.linkedin.com** – Must be done via your profile.

Meetup: **https://www.meetup.com/**

RegOnline: **https://www.regonline.com**

Ticketbud: **https://ticketbud.com/**

Twitter: **https://twitter.com** – Must be done via your profile.

Yapsody: **https://www.yapsody.com/events/**

Yelp: **https://www.yelp.com/**

Your Event Free: **http://www.youreventfree.com/**

HAPPY PLANNING!